Yukio Tsuchiya

FAITHFUL ELEPHANTS

A True Story of Animals, People and War

Illustrated by Ted Lewin

Translated by Tomoko Tsuchiya Dykes

Houghton Mifflin Company

Boston

Library of Congress Cataloging-in-Publication Data

Tsuchiya, Yukio.
  [Kawaisō na zō. English]
  Faithful elephants: a true story of animals, people, and war/by
Yukio Tsuchiya; translated by Tomoko Tsuchiya Dykes; illustrated
by Ted Lewin.
        p.   cm.
      Summary: Recounts how three elephants in a Tokyo zoo were put to
death because of the war, focusing on the pain shared by the
elephants and the keepers who must starve them.
      RNF ISBN 0-395-46555-9 PAP ISBN 0-395-86137-3
      1. Elephants — Juvenile fiction. [Elephants — Fiction. 2. Zoo
keepers — Fiction. 3. World War, 1939–1945 — Japan — Fiction.]
I. Lewin, Ted, ill. II. Title.
PZ10.3.T87Fai   1988   88-6508
[Fic]—dc19   CIP
                                  AC

Text copyright © 1951 by Yukio Tsuchiya
Translation and introduction copyright © 1988 by Houghton Mifflin Company
Illustrations copyright © 1988 by Ted Lewin

Originally published in Japan in 1951 by
Kin-no-Hoshi-Sha Co., Ltd.
1-4-3 Kojima Daito-ku, Tokyo, Japan

For information about this and other Houghton Mifflin
trade and reference books and multimedia products,
visit The Bookstore at Houghton Mifflin on the
World Wide Web at http://www.hmco.com/trade/.

MANUFACTURED IN THE UNITED STATES OF AMERICA

HOR   20 19 18 17 16 15 14 13 12 11

To the readers

Building a world without wars has been the greatest human ideal throughout history. Unfortunately, it has never been accomplished.

Politicians, diplomats, and military men possess the keys to achieving peace. The responsibility should not, however, be left entirely to them when the threat of nuclear war is as great as it is today.

I believe it is absolutely necessary for each human being to work toward the prevention of war and establishment of peace. The power of an individual is small, yet we believe in the strength of collective human energy, just as we know a drop of water is the source of a great river.

For the past twenty-two years, one of the things I have done is to read on television and radio, and to include in my lectures, the story of *Faithful Elephants,* written thirty-seven years ago by Yukio Tsuchiya.

During the last stage of World War II, Tokyo was often attacked from the air. At the city zoo, the keepers, with tears in their eyes, had to kill many of the animals for fear that they would run amuck in the town if the zoo were bombed directly. *Faithful Elephants* describes how three elephants died at the Ueno Zoo in Tokyo at that time.

My act of reading this story seems trivial. However, twenty-two years of tenacious and continuous sowing of the seeds of peace and the prevention of war are now bearing fruit. Strongholds of peace have been built in the hearts of adults and children when they realize the sorrow, misery, horror, and foolishness of war.

The biggest gift adults can give to children is to make public the complete history of and the different viewpoints about war, and to help them consider how we can realize the human ideal.

I hope this book will be read throughout the world and that seeds of peace and war prevention will be sown. I hope that those seeds will soon bud, bloom, and bear fine fruit.

—Chieko Akiyama
Radio and television commentator
and critic
Tokyo, 1988

The cherry blossoms are in full bloom at the Ueno Zoo. Their petals are falling in the soft breeze and sparkling in the sun. Beneath the cherry trees, crowds of people are pushing to enter the zoo on such a beautiful day.

Two elephants are outside performing their tricks for a lively audience. While blowing toy trumpets with their long trunks, the elephants walk along large wooden logs.

Not far from the cheerful square, there stands a tombstone.
Not many notice this monument for the animals that have died
at the Ueno Zoo. It is quiet and peaceful here, and the sun
warms every corner.

One day, an employee of the zoo, while tenderly polishing
the stone, told me a sad story of three elephants buried there.

"Today," he said, "there are three elephants in this zoo. But years ago, we had three different elephants here. Their names were John, Tonky, and Wanly. At that time, Japan was at war. Gradually, the war had become more and more severe. Bombs were dropped on Tokyo every day and night, like falling rain.

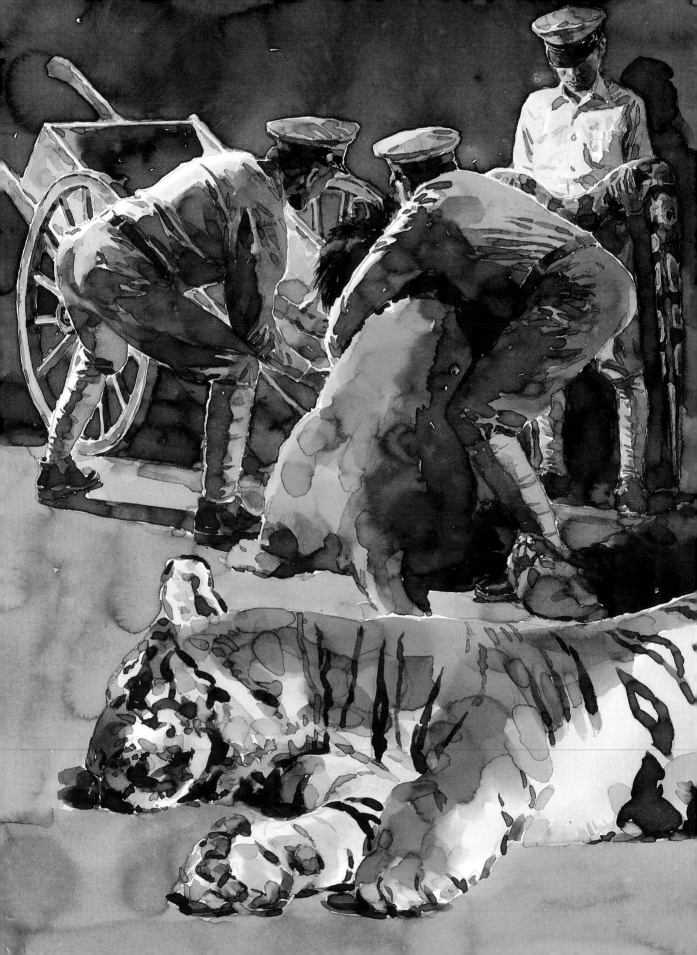

"What would happen if bombs hit the zoo? If the cages were broken and dangerous animals escaped to run wild through the city, it would be terrible! Therefore, by command of the Army, all of the lions, tigers, leopards, bears, and big snakes were poisoned to death.

"By and by, it came time for the three elephants to be killed. They began with John. John loved potatoes, so the elephant keepers mixed poisoned potatoes with the good ones when it was time to feed him. John, however, was a very clever elephant. He ate the good potatoes, but each time he brought a poisoned potato to his mouth with his trunk, he threw it to the ground, *kerplunk!*

" 'As it seems there is no other way,' the zoo keepers said, 'we must inject poison directly into his body.'

"A large syringe, the kind used to give shots to horses, was prepared. But John's skin was so tough that the big needles broke off with a loud *snap,* one after the other. When this did not work, the keepers reluctantly decided to starve him to death. Poor John died seventeen days later.

"Then it was Tonky's and Wanly's turns to die. These two had always gazed at people with loving eyes. They were sweet and gentle-hearted. The zoo keepers wanted so much to keep Tonky and Wanly alive that they thought of sending them to the zoo in Sendai, far north of Tokyo.

"But what if bombs fell on Sendai? What if the elephants got loose and ran wild there? What would happen then?

"Tonky and Wanly, too, were doomed to be killed at the Ueno Zoo, just like all the other animals.

"The elephant keepers stopped feeding Tonky and Wanly. As the days passed, the elephants became thinner and thinner, weaker and weaker. Whenever a keeper walked by their cage, they would stand up, tottering, as if to beg, 'Give us something to eat. Please, give us water!' Their small, loving eyes began to look like round rubber balls in their drooping, shrunken faces. Their ears seemed too large for their bodies. The once big, strong elephants had become a sad shape.

"All this while, the elephants' trainer loved them as if they were his own children. He could only pace in front of the cage and moan, 'You poor, poor, pitiful elephants!' One day, Tonky and Wanly lifted their heavy bodies, staggered to their feet, and came close to their trainer. Squeezing out what little strength they had left, Tonky and Wanly made their appeal. They stood on their hind legs and lifted their front legs up as high as they could. Then, raising their trunks high in the air, they did their banzai trick. Surely their friend would reward them with food and water as he used to do.

"The trainer could stand it no longer. 'Oh, Tonky! Oh, Wanly!' he wailed, and dashed to the food shed. He carried food and pails of water to them and threw it at their feet. 'Here!' he said, sobbing, and clung to their thin legs. 'Eat your food! Please drink. Drink your water!'

"All of the other keepers pretended not to see what the trainer had done. No one said a word. The director of the zoo just sat very still, biting his lip and gazing at the top of his desk. No one was supposed to give the elephants any food. No one was supposed to give them any water. But everyone was hoping and praying that if the elephants could survive only one more day, the war might be over and the elephants would be saved.

"At last, Tonky and Wanly could no longer move. They just lay on their sides, hardly able to see the white clouds floating in the sky over the zoo. However, their eyes appeared clearer and more beautiful than ever.

"Seeing his beloved elephants dying this way, the elephant trainer felt as if his heart would break. He had no more courage to see them. All of the other keepers felt the same, and they too stayed away from the elephants' cage.

"Over two weeks later, Tonky and Wanly were dead. Both died leaning against the bars of their cage with their trunks stretched high in the air, still trying to do their banzai trick for the people who once fed them.

" 'The elephants are dead! They're dead!' screamed the elephant trainer as he ran into the office. He buried his head in his arms and cried, beating the desk top with his fist.

"The rest of the zoo keepers ran to the elephants' cage and stumbled in. They took hold of Tonky's and Wanly's thin bodies, as if to shake them back to life. Everyone burst into tears, then stroked the elephants' legs and trunks in sorrow.

"Above them, in the bright blue sky, the angry roar of enemy planes returned. Bombs began to drop on Tokyo once more. Still clinging to the elephants, the zoo keepers raised their fists to the sky and implored, 'Stop the war! Stop the war! Stop all wars!'

"Later, when the bodies of the elephants were examined, nothing was found in their washtub-like stomachs — not even one drop of water."

With tears in his eyes, the zoo keeper finished his story. "These three elephants — John, Tonky, and Wanly — are now resting peacefully under this monument."

He was still patting the tombstone tenderly as the cherry blossoms fell on the grave, like snowflakes.